Putting An Through Anxiety

**Breaking Free from the Grip
of Worry and Stress**

Louie Giglio

ⓟ passionpublishing

ATLANTA, GEORGIA

Published in Atlanta, Georgia, by Passion Publishing. Passion Publishing titles may be purchased in bulk for educational, business, fund-raising, or sales promotional use. For information, please e-mail info@268generation.com.

Unless otherwise noted, Scripture quotations are taken from the Holy Bible, New International Version®, NIV®. Copyright ©1973, 1978, 1984, 2011 by Biblica, Inc.™ Used by permission of Zondervan. All rights reserved worldwide. www.zondervan.com. The "NIV" and "New International Version" are trademarks registered in the United States Patent and Trademark Office by Biblica, Inc.™

Scripture quotations marked ESV are taken from the ESV® Bible (The Holy Bible, English Standard Version®), copyright © 2001 by Crossway, a publishing ministry of Good News Publishers. Used by permission. All rights reserved.

ISBN: 978-0-9898508-4-1

Printed in China

Contents

intro
duct
ion

**My flesh and my heart may fail,
but God is the strength of my heart
and my portion forever.**

Psalm 73:26 NIV

———

I want to invite you to take a journey with me into the valley where the giant called anxiety looms large—threatening, taunting, intimidating, incapacitating, and paralyzing us with threats of doom and demise.

I know this giant well, and have suffered defeat in this valley in years past. Yet, I also know there is a way to overcome anxiety. I know first hand you can emerge on the other side of the depression and dread, and live to tell about someone who is more powerful than whatever has a grip on you. It's not a quick fix I'll offer, nor a promise that you will escape the fight. But I'd like to tell you about a champion, a giant-slayer, who is on your side in the battle.

Before we take the first steps, it's important that we not oversimplify the issue of anxiety. This giant is real. And it can be deadly.

Anxiety and its cousins—panic, worry, fear and dread—are complex. There are spiritual, mental, physical, emotional, genetic, and circumstantial factors that can cause us to fall into the grip of depression, pulling us away from those we love and shuttering our ability to deal with everyday life. To underestimate the problem, or blow it off with a, hey, shrug it off and bounce back mentality, is a mistake.

You can live *free* from the demoralizing grip of anxiety.

As well, anxiety is personal. I have heard stories of other's struggles with anxiety and collapse that sound similar to mine, yet every person's battle is different and every experience is unique. A "one-size-fits-all" approach isn't going to be helpful here.

But coming to terms with the formidable size of this giant in no way diminishes the promise of God—you can live free from the demoralizing grip of anxiety.

It's imperative for you to know that you are not standing helplessly alone in your valley. God Almighty is with you and he is fighting for you. In fact, he's already taken on every "Goliath" and won!

Throughout this journey together we will set our gaze on him. We won't ignore that a behemoth called fear or worry or panic has its foot on our neck. But we will choose to lift our eyes and see someone bigger and more powerful—someone who loves us and plans to lead us back into the light.

Say *Hello* to the Giant-Slayer

The Lord is my shepherd,
I shall not want.

Psalm 23:1 NIV

We've already established that everyone's anxiety is complex and unique. Your situation is not exactly like the next person's. But all of us have the same hope today—God is fighting for us.

Walking free from panic attacks, depression, fear, and worry is a process, one with many steps and turns. But the key to living untangled from anxiety is not a plan, but a person.

Your hope is not in a formula, although a formula may be helpful. Your hope is not in a set of principles, although truth will set you free. Your hope is not in a prescription, although one may be necessary for a season. (I know this statement might cause some to "deplane" from our journey, but I would not categorically rule out the potential of God using professionals to aid your freedom.)

Your hope is in Jesus, the Great Shepherd of the sheep. He is the way, the truth, and the life. And he is inviting you to allow him to lead you through whatever you are facing in this world.

God understands that we get stressed in life. Dozens of places in Scripture speak directly to anxiety, and hundreds more to fear and worry. Why? Because people have always been anxious, and God understands that better than anyone.

Arguably the best-known text in the Bible is Psalm 23. At the core of this Psalm is an extraordinary offer from God—namely, that he will lead and guide us through every season. Specifically, God promises to lead us through the valley of the shadow of death, that dark place where we doubt everything good and fear every possible negative outcome.

Do you know a valley like that?

Does it seem like someone or something is lurking in the shadows, waiting to pounce and destroy you or those you love?

Do you feel isolated and alone, as if no one understands the crushing load you are under, nor the enemy you fear?

The key to living untangled from anxiety is not in a plan, but a *person*.

Or is your valley less defined—a hard to describe cloud of doom that descends on your best thoughts, turning life into a shadowy mist of confusion?

If so, God is offering to walk with you through this valley. The way out is not in following a plan, rather being led by a person. Your hope is in Jesus.

I know this may sound simplistic and elementary. But it's amazing how many times we run to a website, a friend, a diagnosis or a book when the God of heaven is standing right in front of us. Jesus is the light in the darkness and he's offering to be your Shepherd in whatever valley you are in.

In Psalm 23 we see Jesus as the Great Shepherd, and ourselves as his sheep. Being called a sheep by God is no stunning compliment, rather, a reminder that like sheep we don't see very well and often do not make the wisest decisions. Sheep are not so swift and can be weighed down by their heavy wool. Not to mention they have predators at every turn, a lion or bear or cougar waiting to take them out. Basically, sheep are helpless without a shepherd. And so are we.

The good news is that Jesus is offering to lead, provide, protect, and preserve you through the darkest valleys and most imposing nights. I invite you to call on him right now, out loud.

In Luke's gospel we read about a blind man who was begging by the roadside in Jericho. Hearing a commotion he learned that Jesus of Nazareth was passing by. Without even being able to see him he cried out, "Jesus, Son of David, have mercy on me." Those in the crowd told him to be quiet, but he yelled even louder. Amazingly, Jesus heard his cries above the chaos, stopped, and healed him.

You may feel like God is a billion miles away. You may believe your voice won't even get past the walls of the room you are in if you were to call on him. But, the name of Jesus is power. Call on him now. Tell him you can't see him, but you have heard he is near. Ask him to stop and consider the pit of depression you are in. Tell him you want him to lead you through the valley of anxiety. Be honest with him and ask him to shine light into your darkness.

You may not know how he's going to do it, but in faith tell him you know he can.

Next, we will look at how our personal connection with our Shepherd, Jesus, can reshape our view of the giants of anxiety, fear, worry and depression.

You're *Not* Crazy

———

*I will not die but live, and will
proclaim what the Lord has done.*

Psalm 118:17 NIV

When I was in the toughest stretch of my battle against depression and anxiety, I dreaded the night. I could manage, if only barely, the days, but I hated going to sleep because I knew that 2 a.m. wake-up was coming, and that cloud of doom would be looming overhead. If you've been there, you know what I'm referring to. The walls feel like they're closing in and the darkness seems suffocating.

What's worse is that after a few weeks you really start to think you're losing your mind. You think you're going crazy.

While it may be true there is "crazy" in the equation (mental, emotional or chemical instability that is resulting in erratic behavior or symptoms), it's important for you to know that you're not crazy. What's more, you're not the only one walking through what you are experiencing right now.

The Enemy wants you to think the opposite. He wants you to feel like you are the only person alive who is in this bubble of darkness. He wants you to believe there's no way out… no end to this misery. He's trying to convince you right now that you will never be normal again.

A big breakthrough for me was hearing from a friend about a pastor I very much respected who had shared a message about his battle with depression. At the time, I had never heard of anyone who was dealing with a situation like mine. I didn't realize what I would soon discover as I battled depression and anxiety—namely, that practically everyone I knew either was on an anti-depressant of some kind, or knew someone in their family or close circle of friends who was. I honestly didn't know that our nation was living in an emergency state of crippling anxiety. I thought I was a unique struggler trapped in a world of my own.

When I did watch the message recommended by my friend, and realized this other pastor had similar initial symptoms to mine ("crazy" physical symptoms), a layer of hope was deposited into my heart. Though things didn't change instantly, I knew someone had survived to tell about it, and I was comforted to realize I wasn't alone.

That's the main message for today—you are not crazy, and you are not alone! As David writes Psalm 23 he is facing life-threatening danger, but he is confident in his Shepherd. He describes it like this, "Even though I walk through the

You are *not* crazy and you are *not* alone!

valley of the shadow of death, I will fear no evil, for you are with me; your rod and your staff, they comfort me" (v. 4 ESV).

Two lines in this verse are calling out to you with hope.

1. For you are with me. No matter how deep the pit, nor how dark the night, you are not in this all by yourself. God Almighty is right there with you. I get that you may not be able to sense or see him. But no darkness can hide his presence from you.

In another psalm David writes:

"Where can I go from your Spirit? Where can I flee from your presence? If I go up to the heavens, you are there; if I make my bed in the depths, you are there. If I say, 'Surely the darkness will hide me and the light become night around me,' even the darkness will not be dark to you; the night will shine like the day, for darkness is as light to you." (Psalm 139:7–8, 11–12 NIV)

2. Even though I walk through the valley. God is not leading you TO the valley you're in. He promises to lead you THROUGH it. This current place of struggle will not be the end of you.

If you had told me years ago when I was in the grip of depression that I would be writing devotions about putting an "X" through anxiety…that I'd be in my right mind, functioning in my gifts, filled with the light of Jesus and powered by the wind of the Spirit, encouraging others that they can come back from the brink of despair…I would have thought you were the crazy one.

Yet, here I am. By the grace of God I stand. I say that to boast in Jesus, believing it will inject a dose of hope into your night. I didn't have an instant turn-around. But I did come out of the night and into the light of day. My bout was incapacitating for months and afterwards my anxiety didn't permanently go away. In fact, to be transparent, some days that lingering sense of anxiety still lurks over my left shoulder about sixty miles behind me. The difference now is I now know what it is and I know it's not going to take me out.

And I believe, by the power of Jesus' name, it's not going to take you out either. The Devil may be prowling around, roaring like a lion, seeking someone to devour. But Jesus is actually THE LION KING, and he is with you in the valley called the shadow of death.

Call out to Jesus even now. Call on his mighty name. Thank him that he is with you. Tell him you believe he can lead you to the light again.

If you would allow me, I'd like to speak that over your life today through this prayer: Father, I lift up my friend who is reading this right now, especially the one who feels like there is no where else to turn. I speak the powerful name of Jesus of Nazareth over their situation. Please shine truth into the cobwebs of despair and allow them to see you right there with them in the midst of the darkness. I thank you that you promise to lead them to the other side if they will put their trust in you. Jesus, you are greater than whatever is trying to take them out. Preserve. Protect. Awaken. Restore. For your great glory, amen.

Resizing
Your Giant

—

I have set the Lord
continually before me.

Psalm 16:8 NIV

The Devil is a liar. Lying is what he's been doing since the beginning. Jesus said about him, "When he lies, he speaks his native language, for he is a liar and the father of lies" (John 8:44 NIV).

One of the things he's lying to you about is the size of your giant. Goliath, mind you, wasn't a shrimp of a guy. He was over nine feet tall and towered over the best of Israel's fighting men. Like Goliath, it's likely your anxiety looks a lot bigger and more powerful than you.

The Devil is quick to agree. He's telling you:

You will never win.
You don't stand a chance.

This black hole is too powerful, it's going to suck you into its vortex of doom and you'll never get out.

He's actually telling some of you right now that reading through this journey "thing" is not going to work either. He's saying, *Don't get your hopes up, friend. Things are never going to change for you.*

But, you must remember that when the Devil speaks he never leads us to the truth.

That's not to say your giant isn't real, and big. As you're reading this your giant may even have the upper hand. But your giant is not bigger than Jesus. Let's say that again:

Your giant may be big, but your giant is not bigger than Jesus.

Today, Jesus wants to break the power of the lie that says otherwise, and tell you again that he is bigger than whatever you are up against. The question today is which voice will you choose—the liar or the One who speaks truth.

You have the power, no matter how helpless or broken-down you feel, to choose what you set before you today. You can fix your eyes on the giant, or you can lift your eyes higher to the God of heaven and earth. If you only have the giant in view you will be convinced that you are tiny and powerless. But if you set the Almighty in view, your giant will be resized by God's greatness.

When Moses led the people of God out of bondage in Egypt, God brought them toward the land of promise. Once they were close, Moses sent twelve men to spy out the land and assess the situation. They returned to report that the land was, in fact, amazing, filled with bounty and provision just as God had said.

But, there was a problem. Warriors filled the fortressed cities. As well, they saw the sons of Anak, giants that made them say, "We seemed like grasshoppers in our own eyes, and we looked the same to them" (Numbers 13:33 NIV).

The issue wasn't the size of the giants that inhabited the land. The problem was that they failed to remember the size of their God. After all, God had parted a sea and destroyed the powerful charioteers of Pharaoh, so surely he could manage whatever giants they would face in this new land.

They allowed the size of the giants to get between them and their God.

If you're going to put an "X" through your anxiety, you're going to have to get God in view. That doesn't mean that you ignore the problem, just that you begin with God.

Multiple times God reminded the people, "I am the Lord your God, who brought you out of Egypt." You would think they would never forget. But they did. And we do too.

We forget about the powerful work of Jesus on the cross to defeat every giant, destroying once and for all the power

Your giant may be big, but your giant isn't bigger than *Jesus*.

of sin, death, and the grave. We forget that he created the universe with just a word and sustains all things by his mighty power. We forget that he has promised to lead us through the valley and to fulfill his purpose for our life.

So, do whatever you must today to move Jesus into view. Put him in front of your anxiety, depression, panic or worry.

Let him stand in front of them all. And when he is there, worship him for who he is.

In the summer of 2017, parts of the U.S. witnessed a total eclipse of the sun. For this to happen, the moon, which is much smaller than the sun but much closer to the earth, was positioned perfectly between the people viewing and the blazing sun. The moon blocked out the powerful rays of the sun and created a new atmospheric reality on that spot of earth.

In the same way, worship allows us to choose to move God between our view and our giants.

Move God into view. Praise him because he is greater than all. Let worship become the new soundtrack to your story, replacing the dirge of dread that's been playing in the background all this time. Say again, I will not die but live, and will proclaim what the Lord has done! (Psalm 118:17 NIV)

Choose to see Jesus and make your giant stand to the side. Tell of God's might and make your giant sing along.

No, I'm serious. Get songs of praise playing right away. Set a playlist on your phone or computer. Put a worship CD on in the room. Get your headphones plugged in and ready for when that 2 a.m. wake-up comes. Drown out the taunts of the giants by lifting up the praise of God.

The results will astound you (and probably amaze the doctors). David writes:

"I keep my eyes always on the Lord. With him at my right hand, I will not be shaken. Therefore my heart is glad and my tongue rejoices; my body also will rest secure, because you will not abandon me to the realm of the dead, nor will you let your faithful one see decay. You make known to me the path of life; you will fill me with joy in your presence, with eternal pleasures at your right hand" (Psalm 16:8–11 NIV).

When anxiety is all you see, your songs of God's praise will cease. But when God is in view, worship can flow in spite of your circumstances. When worship flows, things change, because worship is a weapon that pierces the darkness. I know this to be true, because a song of praise in the darkest of nights marked the turning point in my battle and ultimately led me into the light.

The Enemy wants you to keep praising the giant, to keep telling everyone in earshot how powerful anxiety is. But, it's time to pump up the volume on true worship, telling God and anyone listening that you believe that he is greater.

Digging to the *Bottom* of Your Fear

—

*Cast all your anxiety on him [Jesus]
because he cares for you.*

1 Peter 5:7 NIV

If it's not already clear, I am not a doctor of any kind, and would be a fool to try to prescribe a simple Band-Aid of spiritual sounding mumbo jumbo to someone suffering the paralyzing effects of panic, anxiety or depression. Yet, I can offer hope to everyone longing for a breakthrough. I am downstream from many of you reading this today, calling from the other side of this valley—you will get through this. I realize many of you have fought this fight for years, but God doesn't want you to lose hope.

For me, it was important to come to the point where I began to realize my "anxiety" wasn't a thing in and of itself. Rather, my anxiety was a symptom of something else. I found myself saying things like, "I'm not going to be able to make it to work today, my anxiety is acting up again." Or, "I feel like my anxiety is rising up, I better go lie down."

I was acting like anxiety was a cause rather than a symptom.

That's incredibly frustrating because anxiety is a nebulous enemy. You can't touch it or see it, or even describe it well. At least you can see when your wrist is swollen from a broken bone, or see the rash on your face from an allergic reaction. But anxiety, in all its forms, is vague, murky, invisible, and hard to pin to the wall.

Another breakthrough came for me when I began to see that something was causing the anxiety. In some cases it was something deep down within my heart. Other times it was something right on the surface of life. Most often what was causing me to be anxious wasn't a thing but a person. Someone was doing or saying something that unsettled me, or was outside of my desired outcome.

I realized most of the things keeping me up at night were connected to people and relationships. I was spending hours trying to manage results, replay conversations, control scenarios, or protect myself and those around me.

I know firsthand that if you're trying to control the world, or the people around you, you're spending a lot of time staring at the ceiling at night.

But, Jesus offers a better way.

First Peter 5:7 invites you to cast all your anxiety on Jesus, because he cares for you. I love the mental picture of us throwing our anxiety onto Jesus—off-loading what's troubling us onto him.

In the original Greek language, the word used for anxiety in this verse means to divide, or to pull apart. That's what happens to our hearts when we are anxious about something. So what is the offer? We can transfer the worry that's pulling our heart in two to Jesus and find rest for our souls.

Take a moment and excavate below the surface of your anxiety, remembering that anxiety is not a "thing" in and of itself. Dig down a little deeper and ask the critical questions:

What (or who) is pulling at my peace of mind?

What situation or fear or potential outcome is making me feel like I need to manage or control things?

Once you can name it you are on the road to freedom, because when you can identify it you can specifically cast it on Jesus in a meaningful way. You can transfer the weight and concern to his care, knowing he cares about you.

Finally, after a lot of sleepless nights—nights where I was anything but restful because my mind was racing from one circumstance to the other—I started picturing Jesus standing at the end of my bed. I would take a step back to remember that he is my Shepherd and take a moment to re-sync with his promise to lead me, provide for me, and protect me. Once I had him in view, it was possible to resize my named stressors. One by one, I would put them in his hands. I would cast them on Jesus.

Why? For one, he is big enough to manage them (duh). And two, Jesus cares for me. He cares about my well-being and always has my best in mind. Even if he leads me into a frightful, dark valley, he only does so to make me strong in his power and confident in his presence in my life.

David had this advantage when he fought the giant, Goliath. When he was young, David had to defend his father's flock. On occasion, he fought off a bear and a lion, once snatching a sheep from the lion's mouth. He knew that it was God's power that enabled him to do such mighty things, and that confidence spilled over into his encounter with the nine-foot-tall warrior.

Jesus cares about you and wants to make you strong. He wants you to learn that he can be strong in and through you. So when "anxiety" starts creeping in, don't generalize about your condition. Stop and think about what it is that is actually making you anxious. Name it. Say it out loud. And cast it on Jesus.

"Jesus, what _____ is saying about me is making me angry."

"Jesus, I'm afraid of what's going to happen when I show up for this class at school because of _____, _____, and _____. They are taunting me and making me feel afraid and inferior."

Worship is a weapon that pierces the darkness

"Jesus, I'm worried about my son."

"Jesus, my business partners, _____ and _____, are trying to rip me off and cut me out of this deal."

Once you can say it, hand your worry to him. In your mind, place the person or situation in the strong hands of Jesus and ask him to manage it for you. Trust him with it while you sleep. Believe that while you rest he will work. When you wake up, thank him for caring about you and the things you care about through the night.

To do so doesn't guarantee that you will wake up to find the problems are gone. But you will be more rested and ready to start the day confident that Jesus will continue to lead you and bring about the outcome(s) he desires.

Living free from anxiety is all about trust. Do you believe God is able? Do you believe he loves you and cares about you? Do you trust him to work in and through the circumstances you are facing to do what's best for you?

Your answer is found in the cross, the place where God proved once and for all that he loves you unconditionally. The cross is the place where he demonstrated he is able to take any situation and bring through it what is good for us and what brings glory to his name.

Dwell on the cross. Dig down beneath your anxiety. Look up to your Shepherd. Give your worries to him.

"Do not be anxious about anything, but in every situation, by prayer and petition, with thanksgiving, present your requests to God. And the peace of God, which transcends all understanding, will guard your hearts and your minds in Christ Jesus" (Philippians 4:6–7 NIV).

God's Got Your *Back*

—

...your rod and your staff,
they comfort me.

Psalm 23:4 NIV

For a season during my teenage years, the apartment complex we lived in didn't feel completely safe at night. More than once, my sister and I heard rustling in the bushes outside our bedroom windows, and I wasn't taking any chances.

Just inside my closet door was a sawed off, game-used NHL hockey stick that was my ready defense. I was working for the Atlanta Flames, our local professional team at the time, and it wasn't unusual to bring home a broken, cracked, or discarded stick from one of our players. I cut this one off just above the blade and made what I thought was a suitable weapon should the need arise.

One night, my makeshift nightstick served us well. Around midnight one Saturday, I was awakened by shrieks coming from my parents' bedroom. I rushed into the common hallway in time to see my dad flick on the light switch in their room. My mom was standing on the bed yelling, "There's something in the room! Something is over there behind those books!" She was pointing to two or three stacks of books in the corner by the bed.

I quickly moved that way and peered toward the corner. She was right. Best I could tell, during the afternoon as my dad was grilling on the patio with the sliding door open, a rat from the adjacent field made its way into our apartment and down the hallway into my parent's room. Now, the rat was trying to rejoin his buddies in the field, but how?

In addition to my mom's shrieks, the rat was making a high-pitched noise of its own. When I knocked the pile of books over with my foot, the rat went scurrying behind the bed. It emerged on the other side and again found shelter in the corner behind a stack of my dad's *Golf Digest* magazines.

Momentarily stalled, the rat gave me time to dart back to my room and retrieve my hockey stick. With one jab into the corner the rat let out his final cry and fell silent.

Being the classic under-reactor, I turned to my mom and dad and said, "Sleep well," and went back to bed.

My dad disposed of the rat and calm returned.

But man, I was glad I had that stick!

The problem for those who battle anxiety (and I realize I just added to someone's plight by telling that rat story!) is there isn't a stick big enough to defend us from every fear we face in life. But, thankfully, we have a Shepherd who has pledged to defend us.

David said of our Shepherd, "Even though I walk through the valley of the shadow of death, I will fear no evil, for you are with me; your rod and your staff, they comfort me" (Psalm 23:4 ESV).

Every shepherd in the time of David had a rod, a formidable staff carved out of the center of the lower part of a tree trunk. With that rod the shepherd could fight off the lion, the cougar, the wolf, or the bear. With the staff he would guide the sheep, but with the rod he would pulverize anything that tried to snatch one away.

To put an "X" through your anxiety, you are going to have to see Jesus as your defender. So often when we feel under attack, vulnerable, or stressed we look for someone who will take up our cause no matter what. Someone, as we say, who has our back!

We'll say something like, so-and-so is saying things about me, but Sarah has my back!

We all mean well, but can we just stop and think about that statement for a minute? How big is Sarah? Five feet seven inches? One hundred and twenty-nine pounds? Yeah, she's scrappy, but can she really protect you? And what's going to happen if she decides to bail like your other friends? Who's got your back then?

Don't get me wrong. We all need friends who will stand with us through thick and thin. But if we are finding comfort in someone like us, then what kind of comfort do we have?

Some time ago when I was coming through a challenging season, I traveled to speak at a conference in another country. Before the session started, a large group of leaders and conference organizers gathered for prayer in an upstairs room behind the stage.

Afterward, a woman approached me with a word of encouragement. I had never met her before and she knew nothing about my personal life.

I've had a lot of people speak things into my life through the years, some on point, others not so much. But her words shot through me that night. She said, "I just wanted to encourage you...I sense someone's trying to trip you up, but God's got your back."

What she didn't know was that I was spending a lot of sleepless nights trying to watch my back.

I don't need to know your situation to pass that encouragement on to you. I don't know for sure what you're afraid of right now, but I want to remind you, God's got your back.

As a child of God in Christ, God Almighty has your back.

God *Almighty* has your back.

No evil plan, attack, or fear can stand up to your Shepherd, Jesus. And even while you are sleeping, he watches over you. He doesn't just send you into the dark valley, he leads you through it with a rod in one hand and a staff in the other.

So, thank Sarah for being a dear friend. But, relieve her from the weighty role of watching your back. God Almighty goes before you, and follows behind you. You have nothing to fear. His Word reminds you:

"Deliver me from my enemies, O God; be my fortress against those who are attacking me" (Psalm 59:1 NIV).

"Though I walk in the midst of trouble, you preserve my life" (Psalm 138:7 NIV).

"Whoever dwells in the shelter of the Most High will rest in the shadow of the Almighty. I will say of the Lord, 'He is my refuge and my fortress, my God, in whom I trust'" (Psalm 91:1–2 NIV).

Call out to Jesus right now and thank him for promising to protect your life. Tell him you are depending on him to guard your life and those you care about. Because he is with you, you can close your eyes at night and know that he is watching every side, every angle. In fact, he sees your circumstances coming before you do. He protects you in ways you don't even realize. Jesus is for you. He loves you. And he's got your back.

Letting *Go*

———

When anxiety was great within me,
your consolation brought me joy.

Psalm 94:19 NIV

When you stop and think about it, it's amazing that we're not all in a heap in the corner given what is happening in the world around us every day. Our news feeds are filled with rumors of war (and actual war), terrorist attacks, natural disasters, random acts of senseless violence, political upheaval, financial market instability, foreclosures, downward trends, nuclear threats, refugee plights, dictator's decisions, and crippling diseases.

Add to that the challenges we face in our personal world (relationships, disappointments, illness, loss) and you have a recipe for worry, fear, and, in the most extreme cases, a complete nervous breakdown. If we are not careful we can forget that we are not in charge of the universe. And when we do forget, we run the risk of collapsing under the weight of the affairs of the world.

Anywhere you turn for help with anxiety you will find a few common themes. One of those is to relinquish control—to admit that there are a lot of things we cannot manage to the outcome we desire. In other words, there's a lot we are not in charge of in this world.

To admit this doesn't imply that we shirk our responsibility for the things God gives us to steward, or that we fail to pray in faith, believing that God can change nations and history. Rather, to admit we are not in control of much allows us to remember who it was that brought us from death to life in Christ, and causes us to realign ourselves with the reality that he is actually in control of this world.

This is why recovery programs stress the adage—let go and let God. From a distance (and especially if you are in a season where you pretty much have your stuff together) this saying can sound trite. But it's actually as spot-on a prescription as any. To put an "X" through anxiety we have to admit that we cannot manage the actions of people, events, or nations. We cannot dictate (or fully know) other's motives, nor can we make people tell the truth, stop lies, diffuse threats, or right all wrongs. We cannot personally protect and insulate every person we love from pain, or cause everyone around us to make the wise choice.

But there is something we can do. We can put our confidence in a God who is near, and trust that he is working (even through corrupted human decisions) to bring about his overarching plans for our good and his glory.

It all comes down to this question: Do you trust him?

David, who penned the words that opened today's devotion, had lots of reasons to be anxious. When he was a boy, the prophet came to anoint a king from among his brothers and his dad didn't even put him in the lineup. They had to call him from the sheep fields so he could be anointed leader of Israel. Being overlooked by your family can make you anxious.

The reigning king, Saul, was jealous and sought to kill David. He was literally on the run for his life for a period of years. Fleeing for your life night and day from people of power can make you anxious.

What's more:

> David had to fight a bear to defend his father's sheep.
> David walked through dangerous valleys as a way of life.
> David went up against the champion fighter, Goliath.
> David ultimately became king, with all its weight and responsibility.
> In seasons, David felt forgotten by God.
> In battle, David marshaled armies.
> David ruled a nation.
> David was tempted and sinned greatly.
> David had a man killed in an attempt to cover up his sin.

So, we're not just talking about an innocent little shepherd boy. David knew about anxiety and its power to tear your heart apart. Yet he writes,

"When anxiety was great within me, your consolation brought me joy" (Psalm 94:19 NIV).

His consolation was God's presence. We have God's presence, as well. More specifically, the promise that Christ will be with us (and live in us) if we put our trust in him.

Jesus knew about a troubled world. Yet, he makes this offer to you:

"Peace I leave with you; my peace I give you. I do not give to you as the world gives. Do not let your hearts be troubled and do not be afraid" (John 14:27 NIV).

In a world that appears to be crumbling, Jesus is still the Prince of Peace. He is not often looking for the easiest way to get you out of the fire, but he does promise to bring you peace in the midst of whatever storm you are in.

The critical step for you is to set aside your pride and trust in him. We mentioned early in this journey that no two cases of anxiety are the same. But it is a matter of record that a lot of people who battle this giant have high-control issues—those who like to be (or think they are) in control. If you're a perfectionist and a controlling person it's likely anxiety is at your door, or worse, already in your house.

To put an "*X*" through anxiety we have to admit that we cannot manage the actions of people, events or nations.

To fight the giant of control we must dig even deeper. Beneath the spirit of control is the root of pride. "Me" is at the center of the controlling life. This attitude works itself out through phrases like—I can do it myself. I can control it. I'm fine! I don't need help. I am able to take care of it. I'll be OK.

The problem is, you're not OK.

To let go is to bend the knee and admit to God that we are trying to manage life on our own.

God knows that we are dust. He knows that we are frail. (Psalm 103:14). God understands the human frame is not meant to carry the weight of the world.

Freedom comes when we confess our pride (control) and trust his mighty hands to carry the worry for us. This is the full thought captured in the verse we talked about in an earlier chapter:

"Humble yourselves, therefore, under God's mighty hand, that he may lift you up in due time. Cast all your anxiety on him because he cares for you" (1 Peter 5:6–7 NIV).

Focus on the words "under God's mighty hand." Your hands are not big enough or strong enough to keep the world from falling apart. But his hands fashioned humanity out of the dust and, once pierced on the cross, made a way of salvation for all. And, his hand is holding yours right now.

Before we can name what's underneath our anxiety, and "cast" each thing/person on Jesus, we have to humble ourselves before him. So do that now. Transfer control to him. Pray, for sure. And do what is in your hands to do. But leave the rest with him, knowing that's when your rest will come.

Breathe
Deeply

———

So do not fear, for I am with you;
do not be dismayed, for I am your God.
I will strengthen you and help you;
I will uphold you with my righteous
right hand.

Isaiah 41:10 NIV

When you are in what feels like the fight for your life with anxiety, worry, panic, or fear it's important to understand God may work in various ways to bring you healing. In God's economy there aren't spiritual solutions and medical solutions and physical solutions. With God, everything is spiritual, everything that brings us life comes from and through him. For you, getting the right exercise may be as helpful in your journey to freedom as listening to a song of praise. Most times it's not one or the other, but both/and.

When it comes to anxiety, your answer might be as simple as taking a few deep breaths.

Personally, as a Jesus-follower, I believe the ultimate power in life comes from a relationship with Jesus through the Spirit. I find my strength in Jesus through a connection to his Word—which is filled with truth and divine power—and through prayer and worship in the community of believers, which builds faith and breaks strongholds. But I also believe in the common good that comes from doing the simple things that are clear to everyone.

If you read articles or books on battling anxiety, you're going to find some common threads. For one, you'll hear the encouragement to stop and take a few deep breaths when you feel a sense of panic setting in. That's because the "fight or flight" mechanism that keeps you from harm triggers when you feel like you are under threat (real or imaginary). Once this happens, your breathing becomes shallow, or you unknowingly stop breathing altogether.

Re-igniting your breathing has a calming effect.

The American Institute of Stress (yes, we have one of those) echoes this view, "Deep breathing increases the supply of oxygen to your brain and stimulates the parasympathetic nervous system, which promotes a state of calmness. Breathing techniques help you feel connected to your body—it brings your awareness away from the worries in your head and quiets your mind."

It is God who gave us our first breath and it is God who gives every breath (Acts 17:25). So, it is God who can give calming breath to those who are crumbling under the weight of worry.

When I was in the darkest point in my battle with anxiety, the weeks where I wouldn't leave the house most days, I scoffed at the notion of "breathing deeply" to alleviate my symptoms.

"Um, I'm not really into that kind of meditation," I would have told you.

But, looking back, I wish I'd taken some deep, long breaths earlier in my journey.

Instead, I took a pill that numbed my mind to whatever was making me anxious that day. The pills worked, but one day a doctor said something disturbing to me. He told me that long term, the medicine that was helping me not be anxious would end up making me more anxious.

What?!

Yep, the anti-anxiety medicine I was taking would actually cause anxiety over the long haul.

That was bad news for me because just knowing that little bottle of pills was near helped reduce my anxiety. Sometimes I didn't even have to take one, I got relief just knowing I could.

Ultimately, as I shifted my focus to worship and the light started creeping back in, I found myself forgetting about the little pills. And I was beginning to rely more on the calming breaths.

I need to say, one more time, if you need help, get help. My experience is not meant to be a blanket assertion about medication. If you are in an extreme situation please seek help, because a doctor's care can also be a spiritual solution.

For me, I found that there was something freeing about taking deep physical breaths.

You can find any number of helps to guide you to better breathing techniques, and I hope you will, but I'd like to take our breathing a step further. I'd like to add a spiritual dimension.

God does everything in rhythm. And the very best rhythm is the rhythm of his grace. It goes like this—breathe out, I CANNOT. Breathe in—JESUS YOU CAN. This is the spiritual rest that comes from believing that he is God and we are not God; from trusting his life in us to do what we cannot do on our own.

Oftentimes we stop with the "exhale," proclaiming to those around us, I can't. Sadly, our gospel message ends there. I cannot, therefore I will not.

But we must remember the other side of the gospel story.

Christ lives to be and do in and through us what we cannot do in our own strength.

This is why God invited Adam and Eve into a day of rest on the very first day they were alive. Think about that. They were created on day six of creation and on their very first morning on earth God proclaimed a day of rest. Not because God knew they were tired, mind you, but because he wanted them to remember who it was that made the universe and made them.

We must learn this Sabbath rest. We can't keep blowing through seven-day workweeks, worrying about everything and everyone, believing that if we stop for one minute everything will fall apart.

This kind of lifestyle is the result of self-confidence of the worst kind, and the brand of thinking that paves the way to the pit called "anxiety." God-confidence is what we need, the assurance that even as we work and give our best it is God who holds our lives together.

If you are going to be free of anxiety, you must learn to take deep physical breaths and deeper spiritual ones.

Breathe out: I cannot.

"God, I can't manage these people, solve all these problems, face this fear, be everything to everybody, be everywhere for everyone, get it right every time, keep going with no rest."

Breathe in: But Jesus, you can.

"Jesus, you can be the strength I need, you can sustain me, you can overcome my fears, you can do what I cannot do. Lead me, work through me, use me...all my confidence is in you."

Eugene Peterson, in *The Message* version of Matthew 11:28–30, writes it this way:

"Are you tired? Worn out? Burned out on religion? Come to me. Get away with me and you'll recover your life. I'll show you how to take a real rest. Walk with me and work with me—watch how I do it. Learn the unforced rhythms of grace. I won't lay anything heavy or ill-fitting on you. Keep company with me and you'll learn to live freely and lightly."

Staying in step with Jesus helps you stay out of step with anxiety.

As Paul writes in Philippians 3:3, we are those who serve God by his Spirit, who boast in Christ Jesus, and who put no confidence in the flesh. The word for spirit in this verse is the same word for breath. It is God's power, by his Spirit, that makes the grace of Jesus work inside of you—his breath, informing your breath, quieting your mind.

Try it right now. Take ten deep breaths and hold them for as long as you can. With each one center your mind on Jesus. Tell him as you breathe, "I cannot, but I believe you can."

Staying *in* step with Jesus helps you stay *out* of step with anxiety.

Father, thank you for every person finishing this devotional journey. Thank you for giving them the strength to make it to the end, especially those who were afraid they would give up and not make it this far. I pray that you will continue to open eyes by your Spirit so that each of us can see Jesus more clearly. And, I ask that you would give each person the faith they need to take the next step in your power. You have broken every chain that binds us. Give us the grace to clothe ourselves in the light of your truth and love. Jesus, we confess that you are Lord of all. Be praised in us as we cling to you and walk free from anxiety. Amen.

CONTINUE YOUR JOURNEY WITH

Goliath *Must* Fall

I am honored that you have taken time to read this little book. If you've benefited from *Putting An "X" Through Anxiety*, I know you will find *Goliath Must Fall* helpful. I talk more about my personal battle with anxiety and control, as well as other giants we face in life such as anger, rejection, addiction, comfort and fear. Plus, we dive deeper into Psalm 23 and the freedom that results when we find a closer connection with Jesus, our Shepherd.

I believe *Goliath Must Fall* will encourage you to greater freedom as you come to see that Jesus is your Giant-Slayer.

Thank you again for taking this journey with me, and know that you are in my prayers as Jesus gives you the strength to put an "X" through anxiety.

For freedom,

Louie Giglio

Goliath Must Fall
Winning the Battle
Against Your Giants

Goliat Debe Caer
Gana La Batalla
Contra, Tus Gigantes

SPANISH EDITION

Goliath Must Fall
Personal or Group Study,
Study Guide
Six Session DVD

About the Author

Louie Giglio is pastor of Passion City Church and the founder of the Passion movement, which exists to call a generation to leverage their lives for the fame of Jesus.

Since 1997, Passion has gathered collegiate-aged young people in events across the U.S. and around the world. Recently, Passion 2017 gathered more than 55,000 students in Atlanta's Georgia Dome in one of the largest collegiate gatherings in its history.

In addition to the collegiate gatherings of Passion Conferences, Louie and his wife Shelley lead the teams at Passion City Church, sixstepsrecords, and the Passion Global Institute.

Louie is the author of *The Comeback*, *The Air I Breathe*, *I Am Not But I Know I Am*, and *Goliath Must Fall*. As a communicator, Louie speaks at events throughout the U.S. and across the globe. He is widely known for messages such as "Indescribable" and "How Great Is Our God."

An Atlanta native and graduate of Georgia State University, Louie has done postgraduate work at Baylor University and holds a master's degree from Southwestern Baptist Theological Seminary. Louie and Shelley make their home in Atlanta.